*Priests for a New Era* provides a thor[o]
ical and theological dimensions of [
a welcome and valuable resource fo
standing more profoundly what it m                              ... provides
a reflection of the wisdom of spiritual guides, particularly Saint
Pope John Paul II, Pope Benedict XVI, and, of course, Pope Francis.

In this book, Monsignor Francis Kelly clearly exhibits not only
his expertise on the subject but also his devotion to the formation
of priests from his many years as a seminary rector and later as
superior of the Casa Santa Maria.

**HIS EMINENCE CARDINAL DONALD WUERL**, *Archbishop of Washington*

In *Priests for a New Era*, Msgr. Francis Kelly offers an inspiring
reflection on priesthood that will encourage any clergy—both
young and old—to exercise their ministry as servants who accompany others on their pilgrimage of faith. He also offers them practical advice on how to empower the laity through their pastoral
ministry and to celebrate the Church's liturgy in such a way that
they help others experience the mystery of Christ.

**DONNA ORSUTO**, *Professor, Institute of Spirituality, Pontifical Gregorian University, Director, The Lay Centre at Foyer Unitas, Rome*

This book blends devotion for the priestly vocation with sensitivity to modern challenges every priest faces in carrying out his irre-
placeable ministry. A holy symbiosis of pastor and parishioners,
illustrated here by Venerable Father Michael McGivney's found-
ing of the Knights of Columbus, is much needed, and might not
only shape lives for eternity but also begin to build "on earth as it
is in heaven."

**CARL A. ANDERSON**, *Supreme Knight, Knights of Columbus*

# PRIESTS FOR A NEW ERA

## A Ministry *of* Service *and* Hope

### FRANCIS D. KELLY

**TWENTY-THIRD PUBLICATIONS**
twentythirdpublications.com

TWENTY-THIRD PUBLICATIONS
One Montauk Avenue, Suite 200
New London, CT 06320
(860) 437-3012 or (800) 321-0411
www.twentythirdpublications.com

ISBN: 978-1-62785-382-8
Library of Congress Control Number: 2018943226
Printed in the U.S.A.

 A division of Bayard, Inc.

# TABLE OF CONTENTS

# INTRODUCTION

It has been this author's privilege for a quarter of a century to be involved with the ministry of priestly formation—first as the rector of Pope Saint John XXIII Seminary in Weston, Massachusetts, and then as superior of the Casa Santa Maria in Rome (the graduate house of the Pontifical North American College for priests sent to do graduate studies in the Eternal City).

These experiences have matured my convictions about priestly ministry; and my engagement with, and the example of, so many good men who have been called to the ministry at a challenging time have certainly made me a much better priest.

I am happy now to share these experiences and convictions in the following pages. I propose especially in the first chapter to reflect on the special challenges our moment of history presents for ministry. As companions of our people on their faith journey, we need to deeply understand the human and historical situation of our times and the great challenges they present for a faithful believer.

In subsequent chapters, I aim to address some specific issues of living the priesthood today in the light of these challenges.

At the start, however, let me affirm strongly my experience and conviction about what an extraordinarily beautiful and fulfilling life priestly ministry offers to one who is called and who then generously gives himself to it.

Sociological studies have proven this assertion. In one confidential study, ninety-two percent of priests profess great personal happiness in their vocation. Compared to other professions, this is an exceptionally high response, and it was confirmed by other independent studies of priests in different parts of the United States of America![1]

This personal fulfillment and happiness is, of course, an overflow of the joy of the Christian faith itself. At ordinations, it often occurs that the gospel chosen is from John 15—Jesus' words to his disciples as he is about to send them on their mission:

As the Father has loved me, so I have loved you. Live on in my love…All this I tell you that my joy be yours and your joy may be complete. » **John 15:10–11**

As a seminary rector, I used to alert the men in conferences to the experiential joy of priestly ministry: "You will be caught between God's love for his people and their grateful love for

God—not a bad space to be in!" This helps explain the warm affection our people have for a truly good and generous priest.

A 2006 Nation Opinion Research Center study found that clergy are number one in job satisfaction and life satisfaction, more so than in any other job or vocation.[2] Lack of happiness or fulfillment can come from lack of self-esteem, poor self-image, or lack of inner peace. It is the crucial task of priestly formation to target such symptoms and help a candidate to find assistance or decide to not pursue ministry.

A second overarching conviction that dominates this book is the unique nature of priestly ministry as one of "service and hope" as the subtitle of the book suggests.

Pope Francis recently expressed this vision strongly:

> We must never see our ministry as a source of self-gain; rather our sacred ministry has to be the means of our self-giving. And yet, it is so easy for us to choose the flock we want to be with rather than love the flock entrusted to us, choose the ministry we think we are best at or most interested in, rather than the one the Church has asked us to do. Whenever we are tempted to choose our flock or form of our ministry around our own personal preferences or prejudices then we risk no longer following the example of the Good Shepherd. Rather, we have rendered our ministry the means of our self-preservation rather than the ministry of our self-giving.[3]

Also, while one easily associates the priesthood with the sacramental rituals of the Church, one needs to hear the admonition of an effective pastor in the American Church, Cardinal Sean O'Malley:

> In the life of a priest and deacon there can be no dichotomy between our cultic role and the humble service we must give as in washing the feet of our brothers and sisters. The towel should be as emblematic as the stole for our priests and deacons, where humble service must reflect the humble and loving service of the Good Shepherd. Part of our task is to connect the works of mercy with the Eucharist. It is not by accident that the washing of the feet of the Apostles takes place in the context of the first Eucharist.[4]

In this book, I have joined to each chapter the real-life historic witness of a priest who exemplifies some aspect of priestly life. The wonderful reality is that there are so many priests who in a humble and hidden way prolong the ministry of Christ in our parishes, and it is to them that I would like to dedicate this book.

A constant attitude of "service" must inspire not only our interaction with our own parishioners but our interaction with all who turn to us. It is startling the manner or the times that this service may be requested. Recently, a taxi driver here in Rome asked me to hear his confession!

Priests must also serve today in the wider community, being part of efforts for the betterment of people's lives and confronting the real-life problems they face in discrimination or education for their children, etc. This will often require ecumenical and interfaith involvement. Priests must minister to every shopkeeper whose store we enter, to strangers who accost us (as on airplanes), and to "beggars" and the needy.

A pagan philosopher said that "nothing human was alien" to him. That broad vista needs to be ours—the world is God's creation, and everyone and everything in it, therefore, deserves our respectful concern. Priestly ministry can and should be a really rewarding service to the human community.

A ministry of hope! If there is one quality needed in our fractured and insecure world today, it is hope.

Saint Paul, in listing the qualities of a believer, said he or she must "rejoice in hope." He was no utopian dreamer— he catalogues all the persecution, hostility, and suffering he endured in the pagan Roman Empire (cf. 2 Corinthians 11:23–33), and yet he told his favorite community at Philippi to "rejoice in the Lord always" (Philippians 4:4).

At the center of Saint Peter's Square is a giant obelisk brought from Egypt. Carved into it in large letters are the words: "*Christus vincit; Christus regnat; Christus imperat*"— Christ conquers; Christ reigns; Christ triumphs. This is the spirit of the Christian Church in its march through history.

At this moment, we may not have all the answers or clearly see the divine project of salvation fully realized, but we know we are on the right team! Our people look to us to radiate this confidence and to assure them that God is close to them in all their trials and challenges.

The sober reality is that many of the people whom priests serve have, for a variety of reasons, not really had what we could call the "Christian experience." They see the Church as an institution that provides moral guidance—welcome or unwelcome—and that provides rituals to celebrate major events in their life journey—baptisms, marriages, and funerals.

Our pastoral challenge is to facilitate for those we serve the basic Christian religious experience: the merciful love of God, the salvation richly provided by his Son, Jesus Christ, the power of the Holy Spirit who dwells in us.

Happily, many "movements" have helped people have these experiences—Cursillo, Charismatic, Neo-Catechumenate. The challenge remains—perhaps our parishes need to consider small group sessions where study of Scripture and personal prayer can be fostered. These efforts may be among the most important forms of "service" and "hope" the Church can provide and priests can facilitate.

# CHAPTER ONE

# Priesthood in a New Era

Just as "Jesus Christ is the same—yesterday, today, and forever" (Hebrews 13:8)—so the priesthood, which has its source in him, has a certain timeless and perennial dimension. Yet it is exercised in the context of human history and for people who are very much conditioned by the world around them.

There is little doubt that the world in which priests are called to serve today is vastly different from that of only a few generations ago, sociologically, culturally, and religiously.

It seems essential to reflect on that reality at the beginning of a book on priesthood. The Second Vatican Council introduced a new theological methodology in its *Constitution on the Church in the Modern World*, and many church documents since have followed that path: The Council reminds us that:

> At all times the Church carries the responsibility of reading the signs of the times and of interpreting them in the light

of the Gospel...In language intelligible to every generation,
she should be able to answer the ever recurring questions
which men ask about the meaning of this present life and of
the life to come...We must be aware of and understand the
aspirations, the yearnings, and the often dramatic features of
the world in which we live...Ours is a new age of history...
critical and swift upheavals spreading gradually to all corners
of the earth...a real social and cultural transformation....[5]

When the Council Fathers penned these words, they could
hardly have imagined the political, social, and communica-
tions revolutions that have so changed the world! We in our
time need to take their inspired words seriously and try to
grasp the characteristics of our time, which is the realistic
context in which priestly ministry today takes place.

Briefly, it may be beneficial to review some of the aspects
of this new and more secular world. The "Sixties" seem to
be seen as a major cultural turning point in the West. The
Vietnam War and the Watergate scandal stirred anti-institu-
tional feelings.

The sexual revolution that removed sexuality from its
normal habitat of marriage and family life has had devas-
tating consequences on American culture and families. It is
premised on a denial of God as Creator who has ordained
and designed sexuality for his creative purposes. In this view,
human behavior is totally autonomous, and the only ethic is
personal preference and satisfaction.

Socially, we live in a time of rapid change and, therefore, disorientation for many. It is a time marked by digita-

lization, instant communication, and information overload. People are affected by greater mobility, changing jobs, and less stability. Now drones and robots are beginning to do what humans used to do! Migration has come to be an international tidal wave. The challenge to accept and integrate people of different cultures and religions has unleashed a nativist backlash.

Politically, the Western liberal, democratic, capitalist world order that has dominated since World War II is challenged globally by other visions of social reality. Violent terrorism is a symptom of the clash of worldviews, and no country remains immune. In the United States, political polarization is at an all-time high. Our government cannot pursue the common good. Bitter partisanship casts a pall over the political process. Thoughtful Christians sometimes feel that the current system offers them no place to connect.

Religiously, secularism has advanced in Western society. The traditional world of faith where the Church shaped people's lives and behavior from cradle to grave has given way to a society of multiple alternatives, sometimes with a hostile attitude to the Church.

Yet secularism does not necessarily mean the death of religion—only a different climate in which it must be proclaimed and practiced. Charles Taylor, the Canadian Catholic philosopher, has made this point strongly in his interesting *A Secular Age*: "The human aspiration to religion will not flag. Religion remains powerful as a reserve fund of spiritual force or consolation." He notes that young people who have not experienced an "oppressive" form of religion "have a more relaxed response to religion." Many of them are indeed open and searching.[6]

There is no doubt that secularism presents a significant challenge to priestly ministry. Many of its advocates want to push all consideration of God out of public discourse and policy. In the United States at this moment, true "freedom of religion" is under threat in legislation and courts.

In his insightful analysis of the practice of religion in America, *Bad Religion*, Ross Douthat chronicles the apogee of American public religion practiced from the post-World War II era. He speaks of a "Christian consensus" that dominated American culture in those years, which reflected a deep confidence in the centrality of faith and morals. It was symbolized by such figures as the evangelical preacher Billy Graham, who spoke to twenty thousand people a night for sixteen weeks in Madison Square Garden, or Bishop Fulton Sheen, dominating the Tuesday night TV ratings with thirty million viewers. Martin Luther King, Jr., built on that faith foundation to promote needed social change and reform.[7]

In that setting, religious institutions thrived, seminaries and novitiates were filled, and churches and schools were being built at a rapid pace.

That institutional era of triumph and power had its darker side. As we now know, a shocking hidden scandal of sexual abuse by priests was occurring, and bishops, wary of tarnishing the institutional luster of the Church, often did not address this behavior directly or forcefully. This scandal has caused immense damage to the mission and credibility of the Church.

The growth of secularism and concomitant individualism means that religious practice has changed. Parishioners are more autonomous and self-directed. As one priest commented, "Just look at the pews!" In his large urban parish, two thousand eight hundred people attended Easter Mass but on a regular Sunday, only about seven hundred appear. Yet people have not necessarily abandoned the Church or the faith. They still want their children initiated into the Church—they want baptism and First Communion. They want the important moments of their life—marriage and death—to be celebrated in church. For the priest, those events now become evangelizing and conversion opportunities rather than routine rituals.

Not only religious practice but moral attitudes have changed. Pope Benedict XVI in an *Ad Limina* Address to American bishops gave a trenchant analysis:

> At the heart of every culture, whether perceived or not, is a consensus about the nature of reality and the moral good. In America,...that consensus has eroded significantly in the face of powerful new cultural currents which are not only directly opposed to core moral teachings of the Judeo-Christian tradition, but increasingly hostile to Christianity as such...The Church's defense of a moral reasoning based on the natural law is grounded on her conviction that this law is not a threat to our freedom, but rather a "language" which enables us to understand ourselves and the truth of our being, and so to shape a more just and humane world. She thus proposes her moral teaching as a message not of constraint but of liberation, and as the basis for building a secure future...The

legitimate separation of Church and State cannot be taken to mean that the Church must be silent on certain issues, nor that the State may choose not to engage, or be engaged by, the voices of committed believers in determining the values which will shape the future of the nation...a strong critical sense vis-à-vis the dominant culture and with the courage to counter a reductive secularism which would delegitimize the Church's participation in public debate about the issues which are determining the future of American society [are needed].[8]

Given some of the characteristics of Western culture described above, priestly leadership in the third millennium is not for the fainthearted! It is a truly prophetic role that is a service to modern persons who are seeking a path to meaning and happiness for their earthly journey. Yet the priest has to be deeply sensitive to the environment in which he ministers and aware that this new world is inundating his people with messages and signals through multiple means of communication. These messages are often in sharp contrast to the message of the gospel the priest is sent to proclaim.

Pastoral sensitivity to these developments and their impact on our people have led Church leaders such as Pope Francis to speak of priestly ministry in terms of "accompaniment"— humbly walking with our people as they make their faith journey challenged not only by the sinfulness of our human condition but also by all the new roadblocks our culture places on the way.

This sensitivity will require perhaps more from priests than in the past. It will not be adequate to merely reiterate legal censures. Rather, pastors will have to help the faithful develop personal, mature consciences. One of Pope Francis' favorite images for pastoring today is "working in a field hospital." This requires "pastoral discernment" and a recognition that people may be in a "gradual" process of living up to full Christian ideals.[9]

Priests or candidates for the priesthood will need great human maturity and generosity in fulfilling their special vocation in the Church. Perhaps here the prayer of Jesus for his disciples indicates the balance that modern priestly life requires. It is not one of accommodation to this world but of faithfulness to God and his truth:

> Father—I do not ask you to take them out of the world, but to guard them from the evil one. They are not of the world, any more than I belong to the world. Consecrate them by means of the truth...As you sent me into the world, so I have sent them into the world. » **John 17:15-18**

The Scriptures remind us that "one does not take this honor on his own initiative, but only when called by God" (Hebrews 4:4). A combination of inner grace and attraction to the role of service and the Church's external discernment through the structures and processes of priestly formation provide the ultimate assurance of a true vocation from God. This discernment will have to determine if the candidate can confidently navigate the turbulent waters of this "new world."

One feeling called to the priesthood today needs especially two qualities: humility and trust in God. Humility comes from realizing that the outcome of our efforts will be from God's grace and will build on the ministry of others: "I planted the seed and Apollos watered it, but God made it grow. This means that neither he who plants nor he who waters is of any special account, only God, who grants the growth" (1 Corinthians 3:6–7). People are moved and attracted by a humble priest who is obviously not "full of himself" but intent on being God's instrument and truly being present to them.

Confidence and trust in God are the other great requirements. The obstacles and resistance one may sense from today's cultural context require a bold confidence. Walking around the ancient city of Rome, I am often struck by how daunting and hopeless it could have seemed to Paul and Peter—seeing the magnificence and power of imperial Rome and the glory of the great pagan temples—to bring the message of the crucified Savior! We know we are on the winning team and that "for God nothing is impossible" (Luke 1:37).

The following chapters outline some of the dimensions of priestly living that can enable one to cooperate with the grace of God to be of true service to our brothers and sisters on our common journey of faith even in very challenging times.

# CHAPTER TWO

# A Vision for Priesthood

On September 23, 2017, a historic event took place in Oklahoma City. A priest of that diocese, Father Stanley Rother, was beatified as the first-declared priest-martyr to have been born in the United States.

Father Rother had a sure vision of his priesthood. Born of a farming family in Okarche, Oklahoma, in 1935, he was ordained for the priesthood in 1963. He deeply imbibed the ideals described below, especially his identity with Christ the Supreme Priest and Good Shepherd.

As an expression of his radical commitment to his ministry, he volunteered to be a missionary priest in Guatemala. It was a time of political turmoil and violence in that poor country, and so ministry was not only difficult but dangerous. In Guatemala he helped to establish a hospital, supported the local Catholic radio for evangelization, and helped to translate the New Testament into the local Mayan language, Tz'utujil.

Although his name circulated as a target on a death list, he knew he needed to be with his flock. In a 1980 letter he wrote, "The Shepherd cannot run at the first sign of danger." Subsequently, he literally gave his life for his flock.

Any great project, any significant activity, indeed a well-lived life, requires a philosophy, a vision, an overarching dream that energizes, unifies, and gives a focus to decisions and activities.

Priesthood is no different. It is not clericalism to suggest that a priest needs to have confidence, joy, and pride in his vocation. He must be inspired constantly by a high ideal. A priest needs a vision and a sense of mission to serve God's people.

The Church indeed has stated:

> Knowledge of the nature and mission of the ministerial priesthood is an essential presupposition, and at the same time the surest guide and incentive toward the development of pastoral activities in the Church for fostering and discerning vocations to the priesthood and training those called to the ordained ministry. A correct and in-depth awareness of the nature and mission of the ministerial priesthood is the path which must be taken…in order to emerge from the crisis of priestly identity.[10]

This vision does not mean that the priest sees himself set above others, as superior. Rather, a proper vision— one founded on Scriptural inspiration—will see him as a shepherd—one who walks with, accompanies, others in the pilgrimage of faith.

A true vision of priesthood will first draw its inspiration from Scripture passages that reveal God's loving attitude to his people. God describes himself as a shepherd earnestly solicitous for his flock: "I myself will look after and tend my sheep...I will rescue them....I will lead them...I will pasture them....I will give them rest...The lost I will seek out, the strayed I will bring back, the injured I will lift up, the sick I will heal" (Ezekiel 34:11ff).

The supreme model of this vision is the Lord Jesus Christ, the Eternal Priest. The Incarnate Shepherd came to make visible and tangible God's love for his people. Since we were estranged from God by sin, his ministry was above all one of "reconciliation"—revealing the tender love of the Father (cf. Luke 15, the parable of the prodigal son). He invited all to trust in that divine love and to be committed to a way of life based on God's will. He showed tender concern for all those in any kind of need, generously bestowing healing and forgiveness.

This ministry of reconciliation reached its apogee in Jesus' Passion and death; as the Supreme Priest by virtue of his divine-human nature, he became the victim for our salvation, taking on himself the sins of mankind. In Paul's powerful words: "God made him who did not know sin, to be sin, so that in him we might become the very holiness of God" (2 Corinthians 5:21).

Christ's ministry was above all, then, a ministry of reconciliation that changed mankind's relationship with God: "Now that we have been justified by faith, we are at peace with God through our Lord Jesus Christ. Through him we have gained access by faith to the grace in which we now stand and we boast of our hope for [sharing] the glory of God" (Romans 5:1–2). This is the "good news," the gospel, of Christianity.

To perpetuate this salvation, Christ instituted his Church and called men to continue his ministry of reconciliation and salvation. They were inspired and motivated by his supreme and selfless love. As Paul exclaims, "the love of Christ impels us...He has entrusted the message of reconciliation to us. This makes us ambassadors for Christ" (2 Corinthians 5:14, 19, 20).

In one of the more thorough Scriptural studies of this topic, Cardinal Albert Vanhoye, SJ, notes that at the very start, the term "priest" was not applied to the new Christian apostles or ministers because it would confuse them with Old Testament cultic priests. As the theology of Christ's mission developed, its unique priestly character and its implications became clear:

> The New Testament texts present the ministers of the Church as the living instruments of Christ the mediator and not as delegates of priestly people...The "ministry of reconciliation" entrusted to the apostles by God is in intimate connection with the work of reconciliation accomplished by the Cross of Christ (2 Corinthians 5). These texts and others reveal that the apostolic and pastoral Christian ministry has as its specific function the manifestation of the active presence of Christ the mediator; in other words, of Christ the priest in the life of believers, in order that they may explicitly welcome the mediation and by its means transform their whole existence.[11]

Understanding priesthood in this way helps us see that priests are called to bring people the true peace and happiness that they are seeking. No greater contribution to human progress and fulfillment can possibly be made than that which is exercised by the priest truly fulfilling his mission of bringing hope and joy to human lives.

This vision of priestly ministry underscores the reality that it is all derived from the person and ministry of Jesus Christ. Paul constantly calls himself a "servant of Christ," "an ambassador for Christ," "an apostle of Christ." Saint John Paul II emphasizes this truth:

> The priest finds the full truth of his identity in being a derivation, a specific participation in and continuation of Christ himself, the one high priest of the new and eternal covenant. The priest is a living and transparent image of Christ the priest.[12]

Saint John Paul II is here only echoing the faith of the Church: The Second Vatican Council in its Decree on Priesthood puts it this way: "Through Holy Orders, priests by the anointing of the Holy Spirit are signed with a special character and so are configured to Christ the Priest in such a way that they are able to act in the person of Christ the Head."[13]

Reflecting on this transcendent vision of priesthood, it is clear that it is not about power, status, or prestige. It is about humility, service, and self-forgetfulness in letting Jesus Christ and his saving works shine forth. Every priest must echo

John the Baptist: "He must increase while I must decrease" (John 3:30).

Saint John Paul II expressed all this powerfully in a talk to seminarians in Rome:

> Jesus laid down clear conditions for those who intend to follow him: *"If any man would come after me, let him deny himself and take up his cross daily and follow me"* (John 9:23). Jesus was not a Messiah of triumph and power. As a true Servant of the Lord, he carried out his messianic mission in solidarity, in service, in the humiliation of death. Walk courageously behind him...[14]

Finally, Pope Francis, reflecting on this awesome configuration of the priest to Christ and his Paschal Mystery, described above, notes the impact this vision has in the person of the priest:

> He is a man of the Paschal Mystery, his gaze turned to the Kingdom, towards which he feels human history is walking despite the delays, the shadows, and contradictions. The Kingdom is his joy, the horizon that allows him to see the rest as relative, attenuating worries and anxiety, to remain free from illusions and persuasion, to safeguard peace in his heart and to spread it with his deeds, his words, and his demeanor.[15]

The mediating role of the Christian priesthood that has been emphasized here is realized in many ways, especially sacramentally but also in counseling, in leadership functions, and in many other ways.

A full vision of priestly ministry, however, must also include his role as the "sower of the seed of God's word" as Jesus explained to his disciples (cf. Luke 8:4–15). The priest is especially charged to announce and proclaim the gift of salvation and to invite all to "the obedience of faith" (Romans 1:6).

In the challenging contemporary context, the wise words of Pope Benedict XVI can help our thinking about this aspect of the priestly mission:

> It can often enough seem that the priest, the sower of the word, is fighting a losing battle…Yet this parable is a word of encouragement…It teaches us to be full of joy in the assurance that God's harvest is growing in the world and that what is small and hidden (the seed) is ultimately stronger than what is big and noisy.[16]

The vision of priesthood outlined here from the Scriptures and the tradition of the Church immerses priests in the midst of the people to whom they are sent with a heart full of "pastoral charity." To keep this vision alive, priests must cultivate a spirituality and a life of prayer that will sustain them in their service of God's people. That challenge will be treated in the following chapters.

# CHAPTER THREE

# From Vision
# to Spirituality

Father Henri J.M. Nouwen was a priest who was on a spiritual journey all of his life. He was very sensitive, enhanced by his training in psychology, to the human and emotive element of priestly life. He coined the phrase the "wounded healer."

In his search for priestly spirituality, he had many experiences. At Yale Divinity School, he worked with Protestant ministers who thirsted for something of the Catholic spiritual tradition. This author recalls meeting many of them at Saint Joseph's Trappist Abbey in Spencer, Massachusetts—to which Nouwen had directed them. They were often overwhelmed by the contemplative experience. Nouwen himself lived that life for a period, resulting in his book *Genesee Diary*.

Later, he would experience missionary spirituality by spending time in South America with "base communities," resulting in his book *Gracias*.

The last ten years of Father Nouwen's life were spent living as a member of the L'Arche Daybreak community in Toronto, where he simply "shared life" with the mentally handicapped persons who found their home there. Inspired by Jean Vanier, the founder of the L'Arche movement, he came to see spirituality in a deeper and simpler way—as experiencing and sharing the love of God that the Spirit pours into our souls. Far from the frantic pace of academia and from the spotlight of being a lecturer and speaker, he finally found a deeper Christian simplicity and love.

A key to Nouwen's later spirituality was the idea of "the descending way." He wrote:

> Jesus chose the descending way. He chose it not once but over and over again. At each critical moment he deliberately sought the way downwards…Even though Jesus was without sin, he began his public life by joining the ranks of sinners who were being baptized…As Jesus' life unfolds, he becomes increasingly aware that he has been called to fulfill his vocation in suffering and death. God willed to show His love for the world by descending more and more deeply into human frailty.[17]

The context of priestly life in our day, outlined in Chapter One, makes clear the challenges of ministry. In an era of so much frenetic communication and activity, it is easy for people to live a life dominated by multiple stimuli and instant gratification. Such a life can lead to superficiality and shallowness. All of this corrodes the spirit and is a special danger for the priest who must live and function in this real world. Father Nouwen's constant emphasis on spirituality is a needed corrective for "super-activism" that can lead to burnout.

The antidote for all this is a true quest for a spirituality that deepens the priest's character and convictions and orders his life. Being pulled in many directions requires of the priest discipline and fortitude and a rule of life that prioritizes the spiritual over all else. It will not suffice "to go with the flow."

If, as described in Chapter Two, the nucleus of priestly identity is found in the priest's configuration to Christ, the head of the Church and the Incarnate Shepherd of God's flock, then priestly spirituality must include a deep, intimate personal relationship with Jesus Christ as its absolute center. "I call you friends" (John 15:15), Jesus said to his disciples in his last gathering with them. He further expressed the awesomeness of that line: "As the Father has loved me, so I have loved you. Live on in my love" (John 15:9). Scripture scholars Fr. Francis Martin and William Wright help us to see that:

> Here Jesus teaches about the profound love existing among the Father, himself and his disciples: As the Father has loved me, so I also love you. From all eternity, the Father infinitely loves the Son (John 17:23–24, 26), pouring forth all that he is into the Son and teaching him everything (5:20). Jesus loves

his disciples with the same infinite, radically self-giving love: "so I love you." He draws his disciples into this unimaginable communion of love between the Father and the Son.[18]

Humans are made to love and be loved. Christ invites his disciples to the fullest and deepest realization of that human thirst for love. The love he and the Father share with us is totally gratuitous, undeserved. A priest, so loved, should never feel alone, abandoned, or unloved. The absolute foundation of his life is the personal love of God for him in Jesus Christ.

Pope Benedict XVI expressed this eloquently:

> In the call to priestly ministry, we meet Jesus and are drawn
> to him, struck by his words, his actions and his person…
> Touched by the radiance of goodness and love that shines
> from him, feeling enfolded and involved to the point of
> wishing to stay with him like the two disciples of Emmaus
> (Luke 24:29)…The Gospel minister is one who lets himself
> be seized by Christ, who knows how to "stay" with him…
> who enters into an intimate friendship with him.[19]

All this explains the words of Saint John Vianney: "The priesthood is the love of the heart of Christ."

Love not only consoles, but it inspires us to want to share the same saving mission that brought Jesus to this world. The priest echoes the sentiments of Saint Paul: "My one desire is to know Christ and the power of his resurrection and to share his suffering in growing conformity with his death" (Philippians 3:10).

Without a deep intimate personal friendship with Jesus, a priest has a vacuum in his soul. The temptation is to fill the vacuum with other things—pleasures, diversions, internet exploration, unhealthy human relationships, hobbies, travel, etc. A worldly life can ensue, and ministry gets reduced, as Pope Francis warned at his retreat for priests, to "the role of a functionary or worse still a mercenary" who just performs rites for stipends![20]

Avery Cardinal Dulles highlights the connections between this deep personal communion with the Lord Jesus and the activity of ministry:

> The apostolic calling involves two inseparable dimensions: being with Jesus and being sent forth. These two aspects are indicated by Mark's account of the choosing of the Twelve: "He appointed twelve to be with him and to be sent out to preach" (Mark 3:14). They must be with Jesus for the sake of their own conversion, which involves learning what he has to teach, acquiring his mentality, his style of existence and thinking; but they must also go forth so as to meet the spiritual needs of others.[21]

Priestly spirituality, then, is rooted in a loving friendship with Jesus Christ, the supreme priest. "Spirituality" leads to holiness. It is this that our people are especially seeking in the priest—they long to encounter "holy priests."

Holiness or spirituality does not mean that one goes around in a state of pious contentment, as some of the old holy cards might suggest—hands folded, eyes raised to heaven, seemingly impervious to real life around them.

Saint Paul warns us that "all creation groans and is in agony even until now. Not only that, but we ourselves, although we have the Spirit as first fruits, groan inwardly while we await the redemption of our bodies" (Romans 8:22–23).

True spirituality and holiness mean constant daily conversion and sometimes painful growth and development. Holiness is not superiority but humility.

Holiness is basically loving God—giving back to God the love that he has showered on us. Jesus gives us the example: "Doing the will of him who sent me and bringing his work to completion is my food" (John 4:34). Loving God by doing his will—always attentive, alert in prayer to discern what that will means for me at this moment—is spirituality in the "school of Jesus."

At the Last Supper, Jesus the High Priest, says: "Father, I have glorified you on earth; I have finished the work you gave me to do" (John 17:4). That "work" was the Father's will, which meant doing a lot of particular things—preaching, teaching, healing, and training the Apostles. Finally, the Father's will was enduring the Passion. He became "obedient until death" (Philippians 2). On Good Friday, at the end, hanging from the Cross, he says, "It is finished"—I have done the Father's will to my last breath. This is love and holiness.

Basil Cardinal Hume, who made an enormous impact in England, wrote these helpful lines:

There are, as I have observed, at least three qualities in holy people. The first, they have discerned the love of God and responded to it. The test that their love of God is authentic is the manner whereby it overflows into the world around them, their neighbors, especially those who are in need. The second quality is that they have an unbounded confidence in God and in His providence, trusting at times almost unreasonably. The third quality is that they have a positive zest for life. Very holy people are never bored, cynical, unkind, bigoted, critical.[22]

The heart and soul, then, of priestly spirituality and holiness is this deep, unique sacramental bond with the Lord Jesus, this sharing in a special way in his divine love and mission.

Some consequences of this spirituality:

1. *Peacefulness.* The priest is a man so rooted in his priestly identity that he will be at peace with himself and others. He will not need to "prove himself" or call attention to himself. He will be free of ambition, which often arises from a lack of spiritual grounding. A priest will radiate the peace of Christ in his parish community. People will sense that he is "a man of God."

Being peaceful himself, he will also be a "peacemaker." We live in a very pluralistic world. Our parish communities reflect this. It is easy for seeds of division to emerge. The priest needs to be perceived as "above parties"—only concerned to help his people discern and accept the will of God in their lives.

Pope Francis has heightened the idea of "accompaniment" in ministry. The priest is not condemning, cajoling, or dominating of his people, but walking with them as a fellow pilgrim—but sure of the goal of "eternal life in Christ Jesus."

2. *Simplicity of lifestyle.* A danger for priests in Western consumer society is to emulate its lifestyle—to acquire things— homes, better cars, clothes, exotic vacations, epicurean tastes in food and drink.

All of God's gifts are to be received joyfully and with thanksgiving, but we are not to program our life around worldly substitutes for God. As the Psalm reminds us: "You are my God: my happiness lies in you alone" (Psalm 16).

Priests in our culture need to monitor their lifestyles carefully. The "country club priest" does not witness to the primacy of God! This lifestyle can also lead to a deadening of our sensitivity to the needs of others, to our obligation to practice charity and almsgiving.

The assistance of a spiritual director can often be a great help in reviewing our behavior on all these issues. The support of a serious priest support community can also be of great assistance in living an appropriate lifestyle.

3. *Attentiveness.* The intense consolation of ordination will normally gradually be modified as time goes by, just as the first joys of matrimony give way to normalcy.

The priest, like the married couple, however, cannot just "coast along." His commitment needs to be renewed daily. In a later chapter on prayer we shall return to this challenge.

For now, let us note that the priest needs to be attentive and aware that God is present to him at every moment, that the Spirit is leading and gracing him continuously. This is a key ingredient in his spirituality. It keeps him from becoming morose, depressed, and cynical.

To his disciple Timothy, Saint Paul says: "Stir into flame the gift of God bestowed when my hands were laid upon you. The Spirit God has given us…makes us strong, loving, and wise" (2 Timothy 1:6–7).

Deeply conscious of the divine love in which he has been immersed by his ordination, the priest will be a "man alive," attentive to the work of God in his heart and in the lives of the people he serves.

# CHAPTER FOUR

# The Priest and Religious Experience

Fulton J. Sheen, as a seminarian at Saint Paul's Seminary in Minnesota in 1918, made a decision to spend "a continuous hour every day in the presence of Our Lord in the Blessed Sacrament." He maintained this promise for the rest of his long and busy life.

Over the years, Sheen would give many reasons for keeping the Holy Hour: growing closer to the Lord ("We become like that which we gaze upon. Looking into the sunset, the face takes on a golden glow. Looking at the Eucharistic Lord for an hour transforms the heart in a mysterious way as the face of Moses was transformed after his companionship with God on the mountain..."), the absorption of spiritual truths ("theological insights are gained not only from the

two covers of a treatise, but from the two knees on a prie-
dieu before a tabernacle"). "Even when it seemed so unprof-
itable and lacked spiritual intimacy, I still had the sensation
of being at least like a dog at the master's door, ready in case
he called me."[23]

Sheen later further explained the practice:

Very few souls ever meditate; they are either frightened by the
word or else were never taught its existence. In the human
order a person in love is always conscious of the one loved,
lives in the presence of the others, resolves to do the will of
the other and regards as his greatest jealousy being outdone
in the least advantage of self-giving. Apply this to a soul in
love with God and you have the rudiments of meditation.[24]

In his priesthood, Fulton J. Sheen went on to become perhaps the foremost evangelist and preacher of the faith in
the history of the Catholic Church in the United States.
Undoubtedly, the conviction and unction with which he
touched millions came in no small measure from his daily
prayer. Beginning in 1951, he had the 8 PM prime-time slot
on ABC, with thirty million viewers, and this continued for
years. His teaching and preaching resulted in countless con-
versions to the Catholic faith. He wrote a landmark book on
Jesus: *Life of Christ* (New York, McGraw-Hill, 1958). Sheen
had written shortly before his death, "I want to see the Lord.
I have spent hours before Him in the Blessed Sacrament.
Have spoken to Him in prayer and about Him to everyone

who would listen, and now I want to see Him face to face." Archbishop Sheen was found dead in his chapel before the tabernacle on December 9, 1979.

The priest in our modern and post-modern era needs deep conviction and passion about the truths of the faith to effectively fulfill his central evangelizing and teaching role. This conviction is a result of God's grace, but we open ourselves to this grace by our serious prayer and contemplation, by making that the absolute priority of our life!

Diocesan priests tend to be "practical men," and much of their time is consumed by administration of various kinds. As one good priest said to me recently, "I am responsible for twelve buildings." This is aggravated in our day by the amalgamation of parishes due to the shortage of priests, in which one priest may be responsible for a number of complexes.

Yet this problem is not new. When the early Apostles began to find themselves overwhelmed by the administrative and charitable demands of the community, they established the diaconate, justifying this delegation of work by the principle: "This will permit us to concentrate on prayer and the ministry of the Word" (Acts 6:4).

Many Catholics, and maybe a few priests, might recoil at the suggestion that they should be "mystics"—involved in religious experience. Yet, as one recent author has noted, "Mysticism is the experience that gives birth to religion."[25]

It was the disciples' actual personal experience of the Lord Jesus in his public ministry and in the Paschal Mystery that gave birth to the Christian community. Doctrines, laws, and organization all flowed from that. But the fundamental reality was the experience of God acting through the presence of Jesus Christ and the Holy Spirit. The New Testament documents this clearly.

In a similar way, each generation needs to recapture that primary religious experience. Prayer and *lectio divina* (spiritual reading) are intended to lift us beyond words to experience the presence and action of the risen Lord and his Spirit. They are essential if we are to make the Christian experience our own; and for a priest, therefore, they must be the priority of his life.

From serious attention to this aspect of our life flows the conviction and power of our teaching and preaching. The Church itself mandates at least a week in yearly spiritual retreat for priests and encourages regular days of recollection.

The Second Vatican Council says that "the real reason for human dignity lies in man's call to communion with God... man would not exist were he not created by God's love and constantly preserved by it."[26] The mystical aspiration is therefore something already inherent in human nature.

Many have a taste of this when a spectacular sunset or a breathtaking scene moves them. Music and painting can have a similar effect. But these are only invitations to communion with the Blessed Trinity.

The Scriptures invite us to a deep personal relationship with God. They use multiple images to open us to the saving love of God and to surrender ourselves to it: paternal, maternal, spousal, friendship.

The priest, by teaching and preaching, offers what modern humanity needs and often seeks: an experience of the

Transcendent that can give meaning, security, and comfort to our human existence.

If some of the elements of Christianity—organization, ritual, codes of conduct—are a challenge for many moderns—the experience behind them, the encounter between God and humanity in Christ with the light it casts on the mystery of mankind—can be presented by one who has himself shared in this experience.

It should be noted that the proper and dignified celebration of the Church's liturgy can be a major means of helping our people "experience the Christian mystery." Each year in the liturgical cycle we renew the various aspects of that mystery in order to more deeply assimilate them and configure ourselves to the mystery of Christ. A priority for the priest should be to plan and organize the sacred liturgy with serious attention to music, setting, involvement of ministers, vestments, and décor—all with a view to lifting our people up to the mystery of God.

The priest, therefore, has to be a deeply prayerful man immersed in the experience—a man of God, even a "mystic"—who radiates confidently the truth and experience he proclaims. Today, it is not adequate for him to be seen as a moralist, an administrator, or a purely cultic functionary.

Blessed (soon to be Saint) Paul VI already alerted us to this in *Evangelii nuntiandi* when he said that "modern man listens more willingly to witnesses than to teachers; and, if he does listen to teachers, it is because they are witnesses."[27]

Saint John Paul II noted that "we are in duty bound to offer a generous welcome and spiritual support to all those moved by a thirst for God…who turn to us."[28] This, I believe, is the special challenge and the special opportunity that is offered to us today.

Priestly formation perhaps has not adequately prepared us for this. It has been overwhelmingly structured around the assimilation of a large amount of intellectual, doctrinal, theological, and canonical content. All of that presumes the fundamental "experience" and "encounter." But, one may ask, how deeply have these truly been fostered in candidates for priestly ministry? Are they just presumed? What can formation do to make them a present reality?

Saint John Paul II's 1992 apostolic exhortation issued after the World Synod of Bishops on priestly formation—*Pastores dabo vobis* (*I will give you shepherds*)—was a step forward in that it highlighted four pillars of formation: human, spiritual, theological, and pastoral. However, in the actual working out of this, I think that theological formation still dominates the program to an overwhelming degree. This is certainly verified if one looks at seminary curricula and horaria.

Formators need to be creative and proactive in giving greater priority to the "spiritual" pillar of formation so that the ordained may be equipped to provide modern searchers with an opening to the mystery of transcendence.

Could a specific strategy to this end be incorporating into the formation program an obligatory program like the thirty-day Spiritual Exercises of Saint Ignatius, by which he sought to assist candidates to have a deep, personal experience of committing their lives to Christ the King? By first contemplating deeply the mysteries of Christ's life, they are

drawn into a deeper affective relationship with him, culmi-
nating in a free, and very personal, deep act of surrender
and commitment to him. This is the kind of "experience"
that then allows one to share with others the power of the
Christian mystery.

The late Basil Cardinal Hume was a particularly effective
pastor and a compelling presence on television to many secular people in England. Perhaps his own words tell us why he
was able to "witness" and bring the Christian mystery to life
for many people:

> It is easy to get caught up in the "institutional" aspect of the
> Church. But it is so refreshing just to ponder on the mystery
> of God, just wondering what God is like. I think that is what
> people want us to talk about: "What is God like; what does
> he mean to you, what have you discovered? Tell us about it,
> and tell us how to find God." I never cease to be amazed by
> the spiritual thirst and hunger there is in people, and I fear
> that we may not be feeding it. To quench that thirst is one of
> our most important functions. But people want to hear from
> us our personal experience of God and that for some priests
> presents a problem.[29]

A possible solution to this problem is for priests to do some
"faith sharing" with other priests. Priestly support groups
of various kinds have proven to be a life-giving resource for
priests. In them, one can perhaps first feel comfortable sharing one's own spiritual experience and thus become confi-
dent at doing this with a wider audience of the faithful.

Yes, modern people are searching and seeking out someone who can convincingly speak to them about God. Was this not how the Lord Jesus himself attracted people? As Fr. Karl Rahner, SJ, wrote:

> At last there was someone in our midst, someone who knew something…someone who gave a name to the incomprehensible puzzle behind all things—he called it his "Father"—and did so with neither incredible naiveté nor with tasteless presumption. He was unassumingly wise and good. He invited us, too, to whisper into the darkness, "Our Father." At last we were able to know and imagine something about God besides the abstraction of philosophers. At last, there was someone who knew something (about the great mystery) and yet did not have to speak with clever eloquence but with beautiful simplicity.[30]

Each priest is called to both share Jesus' experience of God and to then present it to others with humble sincerity.

To facilitate this, the priest might contemplate taking a full day a month in an appropriate setting for personal prayer and reading—to refresh the experience of God in his own life, to save himself from staleness and tedium.

Modern men and women are seeking God, and they look for a guide who himself has an authentic ongoing relationship with God and can speak to them convincingly about the divine mystery and stir up hope in their lives. This must be at the heart of a priest's life and ministry today. He is called to invite restless hearts to find a center that will bring them ultimate fulfillment and happiness. To do this, his own faith journey must be the dynamic center of his life. St. Paul powerfully expressed the religious experience that drove his prodigious and tireless ministry:

> I have come to rate all as loss in the light of the surpassing knowledge of my Lord Jesus Christ. For his sake, I have forfeited everything: I have accounted all else as rubbish so that Christ may be my wealth and I may be in him. I wish to know Christ and the power flowing from his resurrection; likewise to know how to share in his sufferings....I do not think of myself as having reached the finish line. I give no thought to what lies behind but push on to what is ahead. My entire attention is on the finish line as I run towards the prize to which God calls me—life on high in Christ Jesus.
>
> » **Philippians 3:8–14**

# CHAPTER FIVE

# Empowering the Laity

Being alert and responsive to the human and social needs of one's flock as well as their spiritual needs is a necessary quality for an effective priest. This often means empowering and inspiring the laity in the efforts of evangelization, social action, and charity.

Father Michael McGivney, a priest of the diocese (now an archdiocese) of Hartford in the late nineteenth century, took this challenge to heart in a way that has had outstanding long-term benefits for the Catholic Church in the United States and even in other countries.

As McGivney served the spiritual needs of his people, he was disturbed by their social problems. Most were immigrants or poor or both. If a husband died, a widow would often be left penniless and her children taken away to an orphanage. If a person became sick, their situation was perilous—they would lose all their assets.

Father McGivney assembled a group of laymen to discuss these problems. He felt that, inspired by the Church's social teaching, they should take on this social and charitable challenge. On April 1, 1882, a group of men under his leadership banded together as "Knights of Columbus" in Saint Mary's Church in New Haven, Connecticut.[31] This was the humble birth of a fraternal organization that has blossomed beyond all his dreams to be the leading Catholic lay organization in the United States and throughout the world. Father McGivney, by his personal pastoral concern and practical ingenuity, has left priests an outstanding example of empowering laity for faith witness and work for justice and charity.

It is simply not possible today for a priest to personally address all the varied needs of his community. He must see himself rather as an "enabler" of his people—inspiring, educating, and assisting them to take up their baptismal call and vocation. Already, many parishes have active groups such as the Saint Vincent de Paul Society, Legion of Mary, etc., to provide outreach to those in the parish who may be needy.

The universal priesthood of the baptized is manifested in a great variety of charisms and ministries distributed by the Holy Spirit in the Church. Saint Paul, as a good pastor, already saw this in the community of Corinth (cf. 1 Corinthians 12). He recognized the many gifts present and reminded his flock that these were gifts of the Spirit to be fostered and developed.

At the same time, Paul recognized the need for unity and harmony. So the charism of the pastor is especially the integration and coordination of these multiple gifts for the common mission.

Along these lines, Cardinal Walter Kasper has noted that in the early Church, the leaders were designated not by cultic terms (e.g., priest, pontiff), but by terms that indicated a more functional role for the good of the whole community (*episcopus*, supervisor; presbyters, elders; deacons, servants). The pastoral office is one of community leadership.[32] Of course, this involves ministry of both word and sacrament, which give the inspiration and grace for all to exercise their particular gifts.

Empowering the laity has many consequences:

1. *The priest must be willing to spend time with his people*—soliciting their ideas, respecting their expertise, inviting their suggestions. All this often requires patience; and while the priest may often feel it would be easier and faster to do something on his own, he also needs to remember that doing it alone may diminish his crucial role of "empowerment"—of making the body of Christ function in all its parts.

2. *Evangelization is the great mission of the Church*, as Paul VI powerfully pointed out in *Evangelii nuntiandi*. So the parish has evangelization in all its richness as its great mission. The parish has to have an attitude of invitation and mission. It cannot be closed in on itself or just maintenance-oriented.

The priest will want to imbue this attitude in all who are in any way engaged in the life of the parish. Sunday ushers, for example, can be the first agents of evangelization with simply a warm smile of welcome and a helpful attitude and by presenting the weekly bulletin.

3. ***The whole parish community needs to be "empowered" to reach out to the inactive, the alienated, and the unchurched.*** It can be very comfortable to spend most of our priestly time with those who share ardently in the life of the community. But from the beginning, the Christian community was always "missionary." We have the good news that people are searching for. No one should be excluded—even those still struggling with questions or difficulties about faith issues or moral teachings. My Irish mother used to say, "You get more flies with honey than with vinegar!"

4. ***A priest will be keen to see that the life-giving energy of the Good News is infusing the life of the parish.*** He will not want to impose burdens but lift them. One of Jesus' complaints about the Jewish religious leadership of his time was that "they bind up heavy loads, hard to carry, to lay on other men's shoulders, while they themselves will not lift a finger to budge them" (Matthew 23:4).

Modern life is so stressful that we need to help our people find in their parish experience an oasis of peace and joy. This will mean sometimes that Church canonical or legal requirements are handled in a positive way and that the priest continues to "accompany" persons grappling with them.

5. ***Finally, reflecting what was said in an earlier chapter, the priest "empowers" his people by helping them to experience***

***God, by teaching them how to pray and to communicate
with God.*** Happily, there are many programs and strategies
today to make this possible. Utilizing sacred times such as
Advent and Lent to make these spiritual opportunities available to the parish is ultimately one of the best priestly ser-
vices we perform.

# CHAPTER SIX

# The Priest
# and Celibacy

One of the most public confessions of a struggle for a life of chastity was penned by Saint Augustine (354–430 AD). He makes no secret of the many years of sexual indulgence in which he engaged as a young man—at one point keeping a concubine. As he confesses, he had "an insatiable sexual desire" (*Confessions*, Ch. V, 22).

After years of struggles he movingly described his conversion:

> "I uttered wretched cries: 'How long is it to be? Tomorrow, tomorrow, why not now?'" He heard a child's voice—"Tolle— lege" (Pick up—read). He picked up his New Testament and read from Paul's Letter to the Romans, 13:13: "not in riots and drunkenness, not in eroticism and indecencies, not in

strife and rivalry, but put on the Lord Jesus Christ and make no provision for the flesh and its lusts." He says, "I neither wished nor needed to read further…it was as if a light of relief flooded my heart. All the shadows of doubt were dispersed." » Ch. VIII, 29

By God's grace, Augustine finally was able to master these passions and place his life at God's service as a priest and an outstanding bishop who knew human struggles personally.

Celibacy is a hallmark of the modern Catholic priesthood and one of the reasons for many people's respect for priests. Moreover, in a recent study in the United States, seventy-five percent of priests surveyed agreed or strongly agreed that "celibacy has been a personal grace" and seventy-eight percent agreed or strongly agreed that "God has called me to live a celibate life." As the author of the study notes, "this level of deep commitment and spiritual reflection is impressive."[33]

While Pope Francis has stated the "lack of priestly vocations is an enormous problem," he has also asserted that "voluntary celibacy is not a solution." The Synod of 2018 will, hopefully, examine the crisis of a lack of priestly vocations, but it will do so in the light of Pope Francis' *caveat*. His conviction certainly flows from points that will be made in this chapter.

Pastoral necessity may indicate in the Synod's discussions and in the Church's reflection in the years ahead that, as Pope Francis ruminates, "We must think about whether ordaining '*viri probati*' [adult proven Catholic men] for priesthood in places especially tried by the priest shortage is desirable."[34]

Despite those considerations, celibacy is and will be the norm for most priestly ministry in the Latin Church.

Celibacy is a solemn public commitment that a candidate for priesthood makes as part of the diaconate ordination ceremony. Because of this, the *Program of Priestly Formation* published by the United States Bishops notes that in the years of seminary formation:

> Personal relationships, sexuality, celibate chastity, commitment are essential topics for spiritual direction. In this context (personal spiritual direction) seminarians should be encouraged to speak in detail about their own personal struggles and review their success and failure in living a chaste, celibate life. » **n. 291**

> Seminarians must judge if they themselves have the gift of celibacy and before ordination give assurance to the Church that they can live the permanent commitment to celibacy with authenticity and integrity. » **n. 292**

Celibacy, especially in our sex-saturated culture, is challenging. There is very little support for this commitment. Our culture takes it for granted that sexual satisfaction of whatever kind is everyone's right and that sexual pleasure is perhaps the highest human self-realization.

In this context, the words of a wise priest are helpful:

> Celibacy in our day is extraordinarily difficult. In the society in which we find ourselves, the pressures of the general ethos

point toward permissiveness. It seems to me all the more important that at such a time, we should give witness that there can be love without sexual relations. This is a powerful counter-witness to the false wisdom of our generation.[35]

Even many good Catholic laity do not understand the meaning or value of chaste celibacy. Survey after survey indicates that they would be quite accepting of married priests. Many view celibacy as some kind of penance that the Church has imposed on people who want to be priests. So even many of our parishioners do not understand or appreciate this commitment.

As we reflect on celibacy, the first thing I think we need to be very clear on is that celibacy is in itself a form of loving. It is not primarily a form of deprivation or a suppression or a denial, but a form of loving that opens one to the possibility of a warm and wide pastoral and paternal love for all of God's people.

Celibacy does not stifle the heart, nor does it kill it. It channels our affections to feed and enrich our pastoral concern and care for those whom we are called to serve. People look to their priests to be loving and caring persons. Since they know he is free of an exclusive relationship to one person or from parental responsibilities, they can expect his care and concern to be available in loving service to them in their many needs.

Actually, when properly lived out, this becomes one of the wonderful and satisfying dimensions of priesthood—the priest is caught between the love of God for his people, and their love for God. Again, it is a nice space to be in!

As we consider why the Spirit-led Church has chosen to associate celibacy with priesthood, our first point of reference, of course, is Jesus Christ, our Lord. While being true man, Jesus lived a life of chaste celibacy. His total commitment to love for his Father, and love for the people he came to serve, ruled out any primary or exclusive sharing of that love with just one person. It required freedom from family obligations that enabled him to give himself in total, generous, available love and service to all people—out of love for the Father. By priestly ordination, we become configured to the person of Jesus Christ. As Cardinal Hume once wrote:

> If I had no arguments in favor of celibacy, I would look no further than the person of the Lord—and he was celibate. I would find that totally satisfying. I would say to myself: I do not understand, I cannot answer any questions; it is enough for me that he was celibate.[36]

Jesus' example of celibacy flowed into his teaching: "This is my commandment: Love one another as I have loved you. No one has greater love than this—to lay down one's life for one's friends" (John 15:12–13). Celibacy, out of pastoral love, is an exceptional way of "laying down one's life" for others.

This theme has been beautifully illustrated in a recent doctoral dissertation from Holy Cross University in Rome. The book especially highlights how celibacy can be a fulfilling way of "spiritual fatherhood" in which the innate masculine drive for paternity can be fulfilled precisely in the priestly role. This gives deeper meaning to the respectful title of "Father" that our people give us.[37]

Writing to the first Christians, Saint Paul extolled the value of celibacy:

> The unmarried man is busy with the Lord's affairs, concerned with pleasing the Lord; but the married man is busy with the world's demands and occupied with pleasing his wife. This means he is divided...I want to promote what is good, what will help you to devote yourself entirely to the Lord.
>
> **» 1 Corinthians 7:32ff**

From almost the time the Church became legal in 313 AD, the connection of celibacy and priesthood was affirmed. Already in 310, the Council of Elvira, Spain, and in 390, the North African Council, both insisted on continence of priests after ordination—even if they were already married. There was an instinct that their spiritual paternity demanded a loving availability to all that having further children would impede.[38] This tradition grew and spread in the West and is preserved also in Eastern Churches that still insist that bishops can only be chosen from the celibate clergy.

Imitating Christ in loving, chaste celibacy involves also a commitment to other virtues—detachment from inordinate worldly pleasures, simplicity of lifestyle, and prayerfulness. There is a relationship among all these qualities that together reflect an authentically priestly style of life. Failure in one area is bound to affect others. A distortion of celibacy occurs when a priest uses his freedom from marriage and parental responsibility to engage in a "swinging bachelor lifestyle." His priestly witness, then, is hollow, and he is reduced to being an ecclesiastical functionary.

In considering celibacy, we have to be honest about its sacrificial dimensions. It is not always easy. Above and beyond the built-in biological drive for physical satisfaction, there is the truth that every human being has a need for affection and physical closeness. In times of stress, as could happen in a busy parish life, these feelings and desires can be intensified. One can feel overworked and under-appreciated, and a feeling of loneliness may emerge. It is only good sense to recognize this challenge before these two dangers—stress and loneliness—invade our inner peace and undermine our strength. A habit of prayer is essential—not indeed to remove stress or to banish loneliness but rather to enable us to handle them. The habit of prayer, as already noted, is essential to survive as celibates.

Also vital is the presence of a circle of healthy human relationships that can support and nurture the priest. Experience has proven that friendships with other priests and lay people who share our evangelical values can be a great antidote to stress and loneliness. Withdrawal into self-absorption is never healthy. Priest support groups have proven to be a lifeline for overworked priests.

The final word on celibacy must be a word on love. Celibacy is a supreme witness to the reality of God's overflowing love. The Christ Event—his Incarnation, Passion and Death, and Resurrection—proclaim that the fundamental force behind the universe and our lives is the love of God.

As Saint John tells us, "God is love" (1 John 4:16). This love is stronger than death. The love of God cannot be limited by failure, suffering, sickness, or death. This is the strong witness that the celibate priest gives by his faithful life. It is the ultimate message of Christianity!

# CHAPTER SEVEN

# The Priest as Confessor

On September 20, 1918, one of those very rare visible acts of God's grace occurred to a thirty-one-year-old Capuchin friar, Padre Pio, near Bari on the eastern coast of Italy. While making his thanksgiving after celebrating Mass, he said: "I yielded to a peacefulness....I was indescribably serene," and then suddenly was aware of wounds on his hands, feet, and side. He had received the stigmata—an imprint of the wounds of Jesus' Passion. He was the first priest to bear the stigmata.

He wrote that he prayed the Lord to take away these outward signs "which embarrass me and which are indescribably and unbearably humiliating."[39] His superiors were understandably alarmed and confused, and so the young priest was hidden away and subjected to examinations by medical experts. The scientists examined the lesions but, of course, could not explain them. Padre Pio went on to be a "living crucifix" for fifty years!

Obviously, his ministry had to be restricted, and he never left his Capuchin convent. The one area where he was allowed to function was hearing confessions. This became the hallmark of his priesthood—he heard confessions every day and all day for decades, almost until his death. So many came that the friars had to organize a system of "reservations." Cardinal Lercaro of Bologna described him as a confessor: "He was firm and decisive to the point of being brusque...but at the same time he was so open and comforting that he gave peace and serenity to those who lacked it for years."[40] Countless testimonies have been given of persons reconciled to God and whose lives he turned around.

After offering Mass, bestowing absolution in the confessional is perhaps the moment the priest is closest to Christ.

From the earliest Church, the blessing the Church claimed to offer was the forgiveness of sins. Saint Peter in his first recorded homily said: "You must reform and be baptized in the name of Jesus Christ that your sins may be forgiven" (Acts 2:38).

The Apostles were carrying out, from the first, the special charge the Lord Jesus had given them after his Resurrection: "Receive the Holy Spirit. Whose sins you forgive are forgiven them, and whose sins you retain are retained" (John 20:23).

Two thousand years later, this gift of God is still available through the ministry of an ordained priest, who can say with Saint Paul: "God has given us the ministry of reconciliation...

this makes us ambassadors for Christ…we implore you, be reconciled to God" (2 Corinthians 5:18–20).

The problem at our moment in history is that the sense of sin has been eclipsed. People may admit to "making a mistake" or an "error in judgment" but admitting to having "sinned" seems quaint or artificial. Many have lost the sense that we are accountable to God for our actions. We humans are free, and we are responsible, and so we have to account for our deliberate misdeeds. Saint Paul warned the first Christians: "Every one of us will have to give an account of himself before God" (Romans 14:12).

Hearing confessions is not easy, and it sometimes can be very grueling. One is exposed to the misery and unhappiness in which so many people live. Oftentimes, one can only listen sympathetically—there is no easy solution to their dilemmas.

Saint Bernard referred to Jesus under a beautiful title: "Sweet Gentle Lord of Mercy." The confessional may be the place where people encounter the Lord as such. The priest must present himself as the servant of Jesus and have as his great desire that each penitent leave having received something of the peace that only Jesus can give.

Pope Francis has prioritized this ministry of the confessional and given his own example by frequently hearing confession. In a recent talk, he asked "Who is the good confessor? How does one become a good confessor?" His threefold response is very helpful:

1. The good confessor is a true friend of Jesus the Good Shepherd…[This means] cultivating prayer…A minis-

try of reconciliation "bound in prayer" will be the credible response to God's mercy, and will avoid the harshness and misunderstandings that at times can be generated even in the Sacramental encounter...A confessor who prays is well aware of being the first sinner and the first to be forgiven.

2. The good confessor is...a man of "discernment"...This allows us always to distinguish...to never "tar all with the same brush"...[also to be] aware of...spiritual disturbances— that may be in large part psychic, and therefore must be confirmed by means of healthy collaboration with the human sciences.

3. Finally, the confessional is also a true place of evangelization. Indeed, there is no evangelization more authentic than the encounter with the God of mercy, with the God Who is Mercy...at times it becomes necessary to re-proclaim the most elementary truths of faith...indicating the foundations of moral life, always in relation to the truth, good and the will of God.[41]

# CHAPTER EIGHT

# The Priest
# and the Mass

On July 26, 2017, France was stunned by the news that two Islamist terrorists had invaded the Church of Saint Stephen in Rouvray near Rouen while Father Jacques Hamel was celebrating Mass with a small congregation. The terrorists shouted, "We will destroy you Christians!" and proceeded to slit Father Hamel's throat and stab him eighteen times.

Three thousand people took part in his funeral Mass in the cathedral of Rouen a few days later. He had been a priest for almost sixty years, and by all the reports of him a most faithful, humble, generous priest insisting—even in retirement—on doing baptisms, marriages, burials. All his life, he had been a serious, humble, faithful servant of God's people. Ironically, he was a member of interreligious committees in his area, created after the terrorist attacks in Paris, to promote interreligious harmony.

Pope Francis dispensed with the normal rules and has already declared Father Hamel a "Servant of God," and the pope also dispensed with the five-year waiting rule for a process of beatification to begin.

How striking that Father Hamel was murdered precisely as he was engaged in what was at the center of his priesthood—offering the sacrifice of Christ in the Mass. The Mass is at the heart of the identity of every priest.

At his ordination almost sixty years before, Father Hamel heard addressed to him the words that every priest still hears from the ordaining bishop today referring to the Mass: "Understand what you are doing, imitate what you handle, model your life on the mystery of the Lord's Cross."

As Saint John Paul II noted in his homily at the annual Chrism Mass at Saint Peter's Basilica in 2004:

> At the Last Supper, we were born as priests...The Eucharist and the priesthood are two sacraments born together and their destiny is indissolubly linked until the end of the world. There can be no Eucharist without the priesthood and there can be no priesthood without the Eucharist.

It is to be hoped that this awareness may move the bishops at the Synod of 2018 to seriously address the topic of priestly vocations in the context of their reflections on "youth" and "vocation." The witness of Father Hamel demonstrates the powerful effect of one priest humbly and consciously performing his pastoral duties.

The Mass is the representation of the very sacrifice of Jesus Christ on the Cross. That is why its power and efficacy as prayer is unrivaled. Saint Paul, at the beginning of Christianity, wrote: "Every time you eat this bread and drink this cup, you proclaim the death of the Lord until he comes" (1 Corinthians 11:26). That is why, for example, Catholics want to have this supreme prayer accompany every marriage and every funeral as well as other special events.

For believing Catholics, the highlight of the week is the Sunday gathering for the celebration of the Eucharist, as Christians have done from the beginning, gathering around Christ, the High Priest, to share in the power of his Death and Resurrection, especially by the reception of Communion.

Church leaders, however, must be aware of the physical and emotional demands made on a priest when pastoral ministry obliges him to celebrate three or four Masses on a Sunday in order to meet the needs of the people.

The priest himself must have a Eucharistic spirituality—a constant self-surrender to the Father. The great German theologian Karl Rahner, SJ, put it this way:

> The one total sacrifice of complete obedience…as a falling into the hands of the Father took place on the Cross and is present in the anamnesis of the Mass: it is the sacrifice of the Church, lovingly joining in the sacrifice of Christ—assembled to praise and adore the eternal majesty of the incomprehensible God. This very personal entry into the sacrifice

of Christ on the Cross also continues in actual daily life…in steady fulfillment of our duty…our whole life is ultimately part of this Eucharist as worship of God.[42]

The sublimity of what the priest does in offering the Mass implies a level of personal holiness to which a priest must constantly strive. Saint John Chrysostom in his treatise on the priesthood says:

> Though the office of priesthood is exercised on earth, it ranks nevertheless, in the order of celestial things. It was neither man nor an angel nor any other created power, but the Paraclete himself who established this ministry, and who ordained that men abiding in the flesh should imitate the ministry of the angels. For that reason, it behooves the bearer of the priesthood to be as pure as if he stood in the very heavens amidst those powers.[43]

Conscious of the multiple demands made on contemporary priests in so many aspects of their ministry—not least the multiplication of sacred rites, Basil Cardinal Hume warns:

> We have been asked to take on this responsibility, to handle these sacred things. It would be sad if in our priestly ministry, we ever take it for granted, if we ever allow ourselves to be victims of routine, if in some manner, familiarity breeds carelessness, if we do things mechanically, automatically. It is so easy to become "Eucharistic professionals" until we sit back and say to ourselves: these are sacred actions and therefore are

to be done with all the dignity and reverence which a sacred action warrants.[44]

The liturgy is the chief "school of spirituality." The priest who centers his life on the Eucharist and who takes the time by reading and prayer to enter into this liturgical rhythm of the Church's life as the year unfolds will find himself enormously enriched and more and more conformed to the heart of Christ.[45]

In his Chrism Mass homily in 2008 Pope Benedict XVI asked:

> What does being a priest of Jesus Christ mean? The Second Eucharistic Prayer describes the essence of the priestly ministry: "to stand in Your presence and minister to You." If these words are found in the Canon of the Mass immediately after the Consecration, this indicates the Eucharist as the center of priestly life...what the priest does there is a service to God and humanity.

The priest offering to the Father the saving sacrifice of Christ is fulfilling his most exalted privilege and duty. As the prayers of the Canon indicate, he is doing so for the Church, the living and the dead.

There is no more efficacious prayer! It has been inspiring to me to see how intent dedicated priests are to fulfill this duty to the last day of their lives—sometimes even on their hospital beds!

# CHAPTER NINE

# The Priest and Mary

Karol Woytla had to overcome the threats of both Nazism and Communism in following his call to priestly service. On one occasion, he hid in a cellar as Nazi police invaded the house, looking for young Polish men to force into service.

Early in his life, he discovered Saint Louis Marie de Montfort's book *True Devotion to the Virgin Mary*. It became a fundamental pillar of his spirituality. He made the personal consecration to Mary and chose as his motto, *Totus tuus*—a commitment to be most especially devoted to her. He had hoped to be a cloistered Carmelite friar, but his bishop, Cardinal Adam Sapieha, put a stop to that and steered the promising young adult to his "underground seminary" for the Archdiocese of Krakow.

As Pope John Paul II, he had a prominent "M" on his coat of arms along with his Marian motto, *Totus tuus*. Surely the enormous fruitfulness of his twenty-six-year pontificate owes much to Our Lady's maternal care!

To suggest that every priest should have a strong devotion to Mary is not an expression of sentimental pietism. It has deep roots in a theologically sound understanding of both Christology and ministry.

Mary, by her virginal motherhood of the Son of God, made it possible for Jesus to be the Supreme Priest by the Incarnation. Furthermore, she was at his side throughout his ministry (cf. Mark 3:31ff), even if not fully understanding all aspects of his mission. She was, above all, at the Cross (cf. John 19:15ff), as soon to be Saint Paul VI wrote in *Marialis Cultus*, she was Alma Socia Redemptoris—loving partner of the Redeemer. Finally, she was with the Apostles and the early Church, lending her prayerful support as they began the challenging mission of announcing the Good News (cf. Acts 1:14).

If the priest is configured to Christ for the continuation of the Lord's saving mission in time and space, then his role is similar to Mary's as described above. As she made him present in the world by the Incarnation, so the priest continues that presence when he acts in *persona Christi*.

How much the priest can learn from Mary: total, selfless giving of himself to the ministry; prioritizing Christ and his mission above all else; abandoning himself in unquestioning faith to God's mysterious plan and purposes; perseverance in trial; commitment to the community of the visible Church, etc.

The profound theological reasons for priestly Marian devotion are, I hope, apparent from all of the above. One priest who has spent much of his ministry working with troubled priests (he is also a psychologist) adds a significant insight into the value of Marian piety:

These dedicated men need some tenderness in their lives. I counsel each of them to have some appropriate maternal consolation and some chaste feminine warmth. This is not only possible within the context of a faithful, priestly celibacy, it positively contributes to living our lives with full integrity.

We can find some feminine connection with the women who cross our daily paths, including family members and friends. But with Mary, there is also a real feminine intimacy offered directly to priests and a path to a kind of divine feminine intimacy as well: "We cannot praise God rightly if we leave her out of account. In doing so, we forget something about Him that must not be forgotten, which reveals itself most purely and more directly in the Son's Mother than anyone else" (Pope Benedict XVI). When we lose Mary, the feminine side of God is less visible and perhaps less sensible to us.[46]

Like Mary, a priest's ministry is largely lived out in obscurity and humility. There are no great accolades or rewards; there are daily sacrifices and renunciations—all so that the saving work of Christ may be continued and made present to those we serve. Our lives, then, are very close to hers. We have one goal: that his name be glorified and his grace bring salvation and peace to all. Who could be a better advocate and companion for our life than the Mother of the Savior?

# CHAPTER TEN

# The Priest as a Witness to Hope

On October 28, 1958, a rather pudgy man unknown to most of the world—Angelo Roncalli—stepped onto the balcony of Saint Peter's in Rome as the new pope. After the almost twenty-year reign of the austere, dignified, and aloof Pius XII, it seemed like a startling change.

This author recalls that as a seminarian in those days, we were not allowed to read newspapers. Someone, however, found a picture from a magazine to put on the bulletin board of the new Holy Father. It was from his days in Paris as papal nuncio. In one hand, he had a glass of champagne, and in the other a cigar—this was the new pope!

As weeks went by, the pastoral bent of the new pope became clear—before him, popes did not leave the Vatican. But he went to Gesu Bambino Hospital to cuddle babies and console parents. He went to the Rome prison and reminisced with the inmates about his cousin who had also been in jail. Quickly, an appropriate title for him took hold: "Good Pope John."

A few months after his election, he made the "bombshell" announcement that he was calling an ecumenical council of all the bishops of the Church—the first in almost five hundred years. He said the Church's windows needed to be opened so that some "fresh air" could blow in. He shocked many when he even invited Protestants as guests for his council. His motivation was *aggiornamento*—"updating."

Amazingly, this rather elderly pontiff radiated a calm progressive spirit and a pastoral goodness that quickly enchanted the world. He was a man of hope!

In his opening address to the Council on October 11, 1962, he lamented "the prophets of doom"—"to them the modern world is nothing but betrayal and ruination." John did not live to complete the Council, but it is arguable that without his serene confidence in the Holy Spirit, it would have never taken place.

His hope and confidence in God matured through a long and varied life and priestly ministry and came to maturity as pope. It is inspiring to read his journals and see how this thread of serene confidence and hope grew throughout the years despite many personal setbacks and crosses.

Jesus clearly projected joy and hope, and that certainly accounted for the throngs who followed him. He announced his ministry as one of "good news." "The Spirit of the Lord is upon me; therefore, he has anointed me. He has sent me to bring glad tidings to the poor…to announce a year of favor from the Lord" (Luke 4:18–19).

A priest who is close to his flock will quickly discern that below the surface in so many people's lives are much heartache, misery, and despair. These come from many sources—marital problems, tensions with children, employment dissatisfaction, etc. Often there are no quick or easy answers to their problems.

Unfortunately, the world in which we live compounds the misery. There is great polarization in society, in politics, and in means of communication. Major social problems seem to get worse, government is impotent, and people feel powerless.

In the midst of all this, the priest is called above all to be a beacon of hope!

The central message of Christianity is Christ Jesus—crucified and risen. "It is not ourselves we preach, but Christ Jesus as Lord, and ourselves as your servants for Jesus' sake" (2 Corinthians 4:5).

What does it mean to preach the risen Christ? It means to convey by our words, attitudes, and deeds the certainty that life is triumphant, and that the fundamental force that rules the world is love, and love is stronger than death. It is only in the light of the risen Christ that we understand the meaning of life. The risen Christ demonstrates the power of divine love that cannot be limited or thwarted by human failure, rejections, hatred, suffering, or death—all of which Jesus endured.

We may not have the immediate answer to the sufferings or problems that affect the people we serve, but like "Good

Pope John," we can radiate a confidence in the triumphant love of God.

Because of this confidence, we will be able to listen to people, sympathize with them, and comfort and accompany them—thus bringing the radiance of hope to their lives even in the midst of sorrows and challenges.

We need to reflect the hope of Saint Paul, beset with so much opposition, persecution, and suffering, expressed as follows:

> We know that God makes all things work together for the good of those who have been called…If God is for us, who can be against us? Is it possible that he who did not spare his own Son but handed him over for the sake of us all will not grant us all things? What can separate us from the love of Christ? **» Romans 8:28ff**

We must, of course, not be embarrassed or hesitate to proclaim God's ultimate gift—eternal life! Only then will all the pieces fit together and we will understand God's plan for our existence. Indeed, as the English mystic Julian of Norwich used to repeat all the time: "Yes, all will be well, all will be well." The psalmist expressed our ultimate goal perfectly: "My heart and my flesh will faint for joy—God my possession forever!" (Psalm 73:26).

It is, then, this triumphant love of God that priests must preach and radiate, especially in a world so wounded by despair and hopelessness. Perhaps their whole ministry can be summed up as a witness to hope!

In his first apostolic exhortation, Pope Francis expressed the dream that should animate the soul of every priest:

> May the world of our time, which is searching, sometimes with anguish, sometimes with hope, be enabled to receive the good news not from evangelizers who are dejected, discouraged, impatient, or anxious, but from ministers of the Gospel whose lives glow with fervor, who have first received the joy of Christ.[47]

# ENDNOTES

## INTRODUCTION

1  S. Rossetti. *Why Priests Are Happy* (Notre Dame, IN: Ave Maria Press, 2011).

2  S. Rossetti. *Why Priests Are Happy*, 131.

3  Cited by Bishop James Chechio in an ordination homily, September 28, 2017.

4  Sean Cardinal O'Malley, Homily at diaconate ordination for the North American College, September 29, 2016.

## CHAPTER ONE - PRIESTHOOD IN A NEW ERA

5  Pastoral Constitution on the Church in the Modern World, *Vatican Council II*, ed. by A. Flannery (New York: Costello Publishing, 1975), #4.

6  C. Taylor, *A Secular Age* (Cambridge, MA: Belknap Press, 2007).

7  R. Douthat, *Bad Religion* (New York: Simon and Schuster, 2012).

8  Pope Benedict XVI, Address, January 19, 2012 [Accessed May 23, 2016: http://w2.vatican.va/content/benedictxvi/en/speeches/2012/january/documents/hf_ben-xvi_spe_201 20119_bishops-usa.html] (edited by this author).

9   See Francis, *Amoris Lætitia*: Post-Synodal Apostolic Exhortation of Pope Francis, 2016, nn. 291ff.

### CHAPTER TWO - A VISION FOR PRIESTHOOD

10  St. John Paul II, *Pastores dabo vobis* (1992), n. 11.

11  A. Vanhoye, *Old Testament Priests and the New Priest* (Petersham, MA: St. Bede Publications, 1986), 316.

12  St. John Paul II, *Pastores dabo vobis* (1992), n. 12.

13  Decree on the Ministry and Life of Priests: *Vatican Council II*, ed. by A. Flannery (New York: Costello Publishing, 1975), n. 2.

14  St. John Paul II, Address to the Students and Teachers of the Almo Collegio Capranica (2002).

15  Francis, Address to Italian Conference of Bishops, May 16, 2016.

16  J. Ratzinger, *Ministers of Your Joy* (Ann Arbor, MI: Servant Publications, 1989), 16ff.

### CHAPTER THREE - FROM VISION TO SPIRITUALITY

17  Michael Ford, *Eternal Seasons* (Notre Dame, IN, Sorin Books, 2004), 62-63.

18  F. Martin and W. Wright; *The Gospel of John* (Grand Rapids, MI: Baker Academic Press, 2015), 258.

19  Benedict XVI, 9 November 2011, *L'Osservatore Romano*.

20  Francis, 3 June 2016, *L'Osservatore Romano*.

21  A. Dulles, *The Priestly Office* (Mahwah, NJ: Paulist Press, NY; 1997), 63.

22  B. Hume, *Light in the Lord: Reflections on the Priesthood* (Collegeville, MN: The Liturgical Press, 1993), 150.

## CHAPTER FOUR - THE PRIEST AND RELIGIOUS EXPERIENCE

23 Thomas C. Reeves, *America's Bishop* (San Francisco: Encounter Books, 2001), 36.

24 Fulton J. Sheen, *The Holy Hour* (Washington, DC: National Council of Catholic Men, 1946), 3.

25 Bernardo Olivera, *The Sun at Midnight* (Collegeville, MN: The Liturgical Press, 2012), 3.

26 *Gaudium et spes*, 19.

27 Bl. Paul VI, *Evangelii nuntiandi*, n. 41.

28 St. John Paul II, *Vita consecrata*, n. 103.

29 B. Hume, *Light in the Lord*, 50.

30 K. Rahner, *The Eternal Year* (Montreal: Palm Press, 1964), 97.

## CHAPTER FIVE - EMPOWERING THE LAITY

31 D. Brinkley and J. Foster, *Parish Priest* (New York: HarperCollins, 2006), p. 124.

32 W. Kasper, "A New Dogmatic Outlook on the Priestly Ministry" in *The Identity of the Priest* (New York: Paulist Press, 1969), 20-33.

## CHAPTER SIX - THE PRIEST AND CELIBACY

33 S. Rossetti, *Priests Are Happy*, 106.

34 Both quotations are from an interview by Pope Francis of 9 March 2017 in *Die Zeit* Magazine.

35 B. Hume, *Light in the Lord*, 36.

36 B. Hume, *Light in the Lord*, 36.

37 C. Griffin, *Supernatural Fatherhood through Priestly Celibacy* (Rome, February 20, 2011).

38 Cf. A. Stickler, *The Case for Clerical Celibacy* (San Francisco: Ignatius Press, 1995).

**CHAPTER SEVEN - THE PRIEST AS CONFESSOR**

39 F. Napolitan, *Padre Pio of Pietrelcina* (Dublin: Columba Press 2015), 26.
40 F. Napolitan, *Padre Pio of Pietrelcina*.
41 Francis, Address to the Participants in a Course sponsored by the Apostolic Penitentiary, 17 March 2017.

**CHAPTER EIGHT - THE PRIEST AND THE MASS**

42 K. Rahner, SJ, *The Priesthood* (New York: Seabury Press, 1973), 211.
43 Cited by A. Nichols, *Holy Order: Apostolic Priesthood from the New Testament to the Second Vatican Council* (Dublin: Veritas Press, 1990), 63.
44 B. Hume, *Light in the Lord*, 104.
45 F. Kelly, *Through the Church Year* (Notre Dame, IN: Ave Maria Press, 2009).

**CHAPTER NINE - THE PRIEST AND MARY**

46 S. Rossetti, *Behold Your Mother: Priests Speak about Mary* (Notre Dame, IN: Ave Maria Press, 2007), 17-18.

**CHAPTER TEN - THE PRIEST AS A WITNESS TO HOPE**

47 Pope Francis, *Evangelii Gaudium*, 10.